# Josephine Trott

# MELODIOUS DOUBLE-STOPS

Book I

transcribed for viola
by Jane Daniel

ED 4167
First printing: August 2004

ISBN 978-0-634-06450-0

# G. SCHIRMER, Inc.

DISTRIBUTED BY
HAL•LEONARD®
CORPORATION
7777 W. BLUEMOUND RD. P.O. BOX 13819 MILWAUKEE, WI 53213

# MELODIOUS DOUBLE-STOPS

Josephine Trott
Transcribed by Jane Daniel

In the first eight exercises one of the
two notes is invariably an open string.

Do not lift fingers until necessary.

4

**Commodo**

12

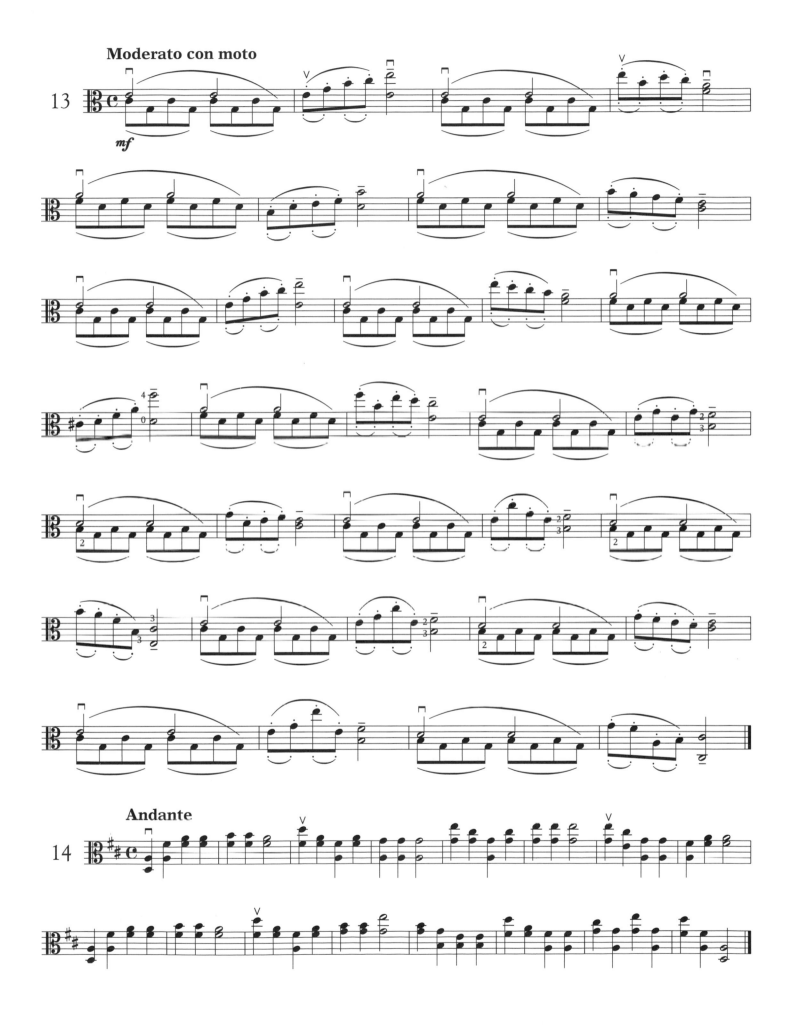

**Allegro moderato**

17

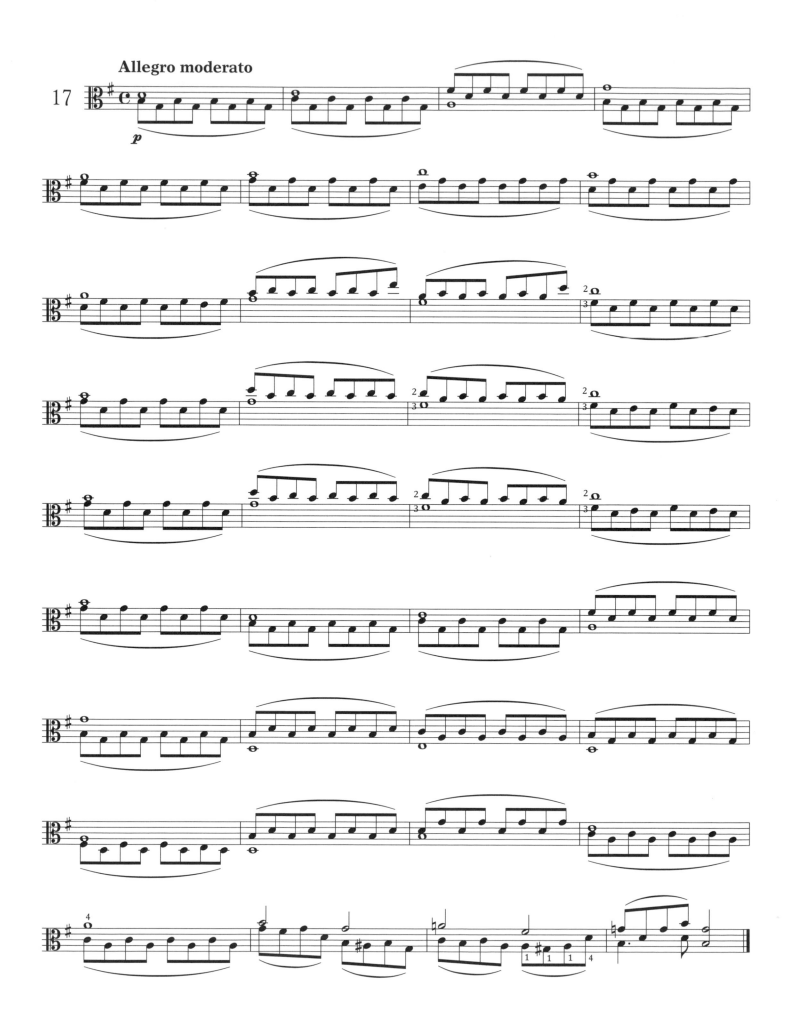

18

28    Con grazia

*+ = left hand pizzicato

**Allegro risoluto**

30